New, Revised Edition

Stolen Property Returned

Your Personal Restoration Mandate

by
John Avanzini

Harrison House
Tulsa, Oklahoma

New, Revised Edition
Stolen Property Returned —
Your Personal Restoration Mandate

ISBN: 0-89274-598-3

Stolen Property Returned was first published in 1984 and
now has over 220,000 copies in print.

Harrison House
P.O. Box 35035
Tulsa, Oklahoma 74153

I dedicate this book
to my son,
John Howard Avanzini,
who has the potential
to take back much of what
the devil has stolen from the Church.

Contents

Introduction

Every minister of the gospel who has received a formal Bible school education has learned about the Law of Retribution. While they have all learned about it, few if any ever teach it to others.

Now, don't let the big name "Law of Retribution" throw you. It is nothing more than God's instructions on how to handle those who steal from you or cause you loss. This book is about that law. It is the spiritual application of God's instructions to Israel.

No doubt you know we are to use everything that took place in the Old Testament as an example for our instruction.

> **Now all these things happened unto them for ensamples: and they are written for our admonition, upon whom the ends of the world are come.**
> **1 Corinthians 10:11**

While the Old Testament deals primarily with natural events, each of its examples has deep spiritual application as well. The Law of Retribution is no exception. It deals with the handling of robberies and losses in the natural realm. However, its meaning goes much deeper. **This book takes you past the surface operation of the Mosaic Law to the spiritual root of every robbery.**

The Book of Daniel teaches that the heavens rule over the things that take place on earth (Daniel 4:26). From this we know that the real motivation behind every robbery comes from the spirit world. It is common knowledge that two different powers are at war in the heavenly realm. One of them is the power of God, and the other is the power of Satan.

As you know, knowledge and revelation increase over a period of time. For that reason, I have completely revised this book from its original 1984 edition. I have also added two powerful chapters to it. I am convinced that with this thorough revision, the book is even more potent than it was in its original form. After reading it, **you will know how to deal effectively with every robbery at its point of origin, and how to get back your stolen property fast.**

I hope you are ready, for you are about to lay hold on some hot information! This information will put the devil to flight and cause you to easily reclaim everything he has ever stolen from you.

John Avanzini

1

You Have Been Ripped Off

This book exposes the most successful thief in the history of the universe. It tells you how to overcome him, and how to make him pay back everything he owes you.

The thief I speak of is a deceptive, calculating plunderer who has moved freely in and out of our lives. This ruthless destroyer has defrauded or robbed every individual on the face of this planet. His bag of tricks includes a full array of temptations to lure people into his power. He tries not only to steal their money, but also to rob them of their relationships, peace of mind, health, as well as physical possessions.

Because of his successful robberies, the wicked now control most of the wealth of the world, and they are using it to finance the kingdom of darkness instead of the Kingdom of Light.

Ripped Off Means "Ripped Off"

You may think I choose the term *ripped off* because I am trying to use modern language. However, my choice of this phrase has nothing to do with modern language. When someone steals your possessions, it causes a painful, ripping sensation that hurts all the way down into the core of your being. There is no better way to put it. **You have been ripped off!**

The most common reaction of robbery victims, particularly if the theft occurs in their own home, is one of disbelief, shock, and inner pain. It is a feeling of utter hopelessness.

Make no mistake about it. Robbery is a personal violation of your private life. When a thief deprives you of your goods by any means, forceful or deceptive, he has ripped you off.

Everyone Is a Victim

By now you may be wondering what all this talk about robbery and being ripped off has to do with you. You may say you have never been robbed.

Well, let me put it this way. I've never met a Christian who hasn't been hit by this gangster. He has stolen some possessions from every one of us. In fact, I am convinced that **most Christians have no idea of the magnitude of the robberies this rip-off artist has pulled off!**

It's the Devil

I will not hold you in suspense any longer. No doubt you have already guessed who this master criminal is. He is the devil himself! He has taken more loot in his reign of terror than any crook in history.

Satan has stolen billions upon billions of dollars from the children of God during the past two thousand years. Worst of all, these robberies are still occurring everywhere you look.

How many Christians have made what seemed to be a good investment, only to watch it go bad? How many have gone off on their own to form some sort of new company, only to see it fail? How many have done what they believed to be God's will, only to lose everything? Just in those three areas alone, I have no doubt mentioned something that has affected your life or the life of someone close to you.

God Doesn't Want You to Lose

Every day I hear stories of financial disaster. How often my wife and I have helped piece back together the shattered lives of families who faced this type of trauma. We have spent many hours trying to help people who have lost everything — cars, homes, money, a good name. So often these bewildered Christians will say something like, "Maybe God wanted us to lose everything so that we could learn to trust Him more."

That is a lie straight out of hell! You can be sure of this one thing. **God will never rip off His beloved children just to make a point!** A careful examination of their lives always reveals some lie the devil got these folks to believe, a lie that opened the door and allowed the thief to make off with their goods.

Are you beginning to see what Satan is doing? Is it now a bit easier for you to understand that he is the one who has ripped off your possessions?

Take Action Now

It is time for you to serve notice on the devil. He has robbed you long enough. For too long he has stripped and plundered your goods. Enough is enough! Don't allow him to diminish your quality of life a day longer. You can stop the devil from taking your belongings, and you can stop him now! **It's time for you to take a stand!**

The next few chapters of this book will show you how to use the Word of God to put an immediate stop to all the robberies in your life. I want you to say this with me. Yes, I want you to say it out loud. "I'm mad at the devil, and I'm not going to take it anymore! From this day on I will start taking back everything he has stolen from me!"

These choice words will start a righteous fire in your bones! Repeat them several times before going on to the next chapter.

2

Prepare to Take Back What Satan Has Stolen

When he is preparing for a fight, a world-class boxing champion will choose a sparring partner who uses the same style and techniques as his upcoming opponent. If his challenger leads with his left hand, he will choose a sparring partner who leads with his left. A wise fighter always wants the advantage of being familiar with his challenger's method of attack. Champions never want any surprises once the battle has begun.

In the realm of spiritual warfare, it is even more important to understand how the enemy is going to operate. When you know his method of operation and plan of attack, you immediately have the advantage. With this vital information, you can easily break his grip on your possessions.

The Method of Your Enemy

The main tactic of the devil is deception. The more you understand about this strategy, the easier it will be for you to protect yourself. The Bible tells us we can know his tricks (devices).

> ... we are not ignorant of his devices.
> 2 Corinthians 2:11

The following scriptures will help you understand even better his method of operation. However, you must be careful when reading these verses. A large part of the truth they convey is hidden from view because of the way the scholars translated them from the original language.

> **And then shall that Wicked be revealed, whom the Lord shall consume with the spirit of his mouth, and shall destroy with the brightness of his coming:**
>
> **Even him, whose coming is after the working of Satan with all power and signs and lying wonders.**
>
> **2 Thessalonians 2:8,9**

Throughout the *King James Version* of the New Testament, the writers almost always translated the Greek word *kai* into the English word *and*. However, the Greek word *kai* has several meanings. Many times it is better translated as our English word *even*. In the preceding verses where you read "and signs and lying wonders," the translation should have been "*even* signs, *even* lying wonders." Furthermore, the proper translation of the words "with all power" is "with all the power Satan has."

The apostle wasn't trying to tell us how strong the devil is. He was exposing the kind of power the wicked one will use when he reveals himself. He will operate in the same way the devil does. He will use false signs and fake wonders. Paul is saying these deceptions are "all the power Satan has," or better said, the best weapon he's got.

If you will allow me to paraphrase verse 9 for you, I believe the original meaning will immediately become clear: "Even him whose coming is after the working of Satan, with all the power Satan has, *even [kai]* signs, *even [kai]* lying wonders [not true signs and wonders, but deceptive or fake signs and wonders]."

I cannot overemphasize the importance of your grasping this next statement. Satan is not the powerful prince of darkness that a quick reading of these verses in the King James translation might suggest. **Satan does not have all power.**

Nothing to Fear

Please hear this truth with the ears of understanding. **You have no reason to fear Satan's power.** Jesus severely limited his ability when He triumphed over him in His resurrection from the dead. The devil now operates primarily in only three areas. He has the power to deceive, the power to accuse, and the power to tempt.

When you fear Satan's power, you open the door to him. Job tells us he lost his family and fortune because of the fear he allowed to enter his mind.

> . . . the thing which I greatly feared is come
> upon me, and that which I was afraid of is come
> unto me.
>
> **Job 3:25**

If he can transfer even an ounce of fear into your mind, the devil immediately has the advantage over you. However, it's an edge that you and you alone can give him. He cannot cause fear to remain in your mind, because you can easily cast it down by the power you have in the name of Jesus.

When the boxer knows his opponent drops his left hand every time he throws his right, that critical information is all he needs to knock the poor fellow senseless. Satan will use fear in that same way. If you accept it, you have given him the advantage he is seeking.

Child of God, you will not move into the next dimension God has planned for the Church until you come into the full realization of your power over Satan. You must become totally aware of your authority to take back, reclaim, and restore everything the devil has taken from you.

Let me now share with you two powerful keys that will give you a distinct advantage over the devil.

Key #1 — Absolute Power

The statement I am about to make is one of the most powerful keys for overcoming the devil. If you are able to absorb the following truth into your mind, you will take a giant step toward rendering Satan powerless against you.

The only absolute power left on this earth is the power of God which now dwells in you. When the Church allows this power to burst forth, we will quickly change the kingdoms of this world into the Kingdom of our God. Observe closely how the Apostle Paul described this power.

> . . . having the eyes of your heart flooded with light, so that you can know and understand the hope to which He has called you, and how rich is His glorious inheritance in the saints (His set-apart ones),
> And [so that you can know and understand] what is THE IMMEASURABLE AND UNLIMITED AND SURPASSING GREATNESS OF HIS POWER IN AND FOR US who believe, as demonstrated in the working of His mighty strength,

**Which He exerted in Christ when He raised
Him from the dead and seated Him at His [own]
right hand in the heavenly [places].
Ephesians 1:18-20, Amplified**

I hope you understand what you just read. The Father of Glory wants you to become fully conscious of the exceeding greatness of His power. Please notice that it is the very same power He used to raise Jesus from the dead, and He wants to release that power in and through you.

Pay close attention. **God wants to empower you with His mighty power!** When Christians fully realize this truth, the Church will quickly grow into the overcoming force God has called it to be!

The day is now upon us when the intimidation that affected past generations must go. It is now time for us to start intimidating the devil. Our old, worn out, loser mentality must become a thing of the past. Why don't we just throw it in the garbage can where it belongs?

We must boldly begin to take hold of the power God has given us. It is time to stop confessing the devil's dominance over us and start telling him to back off. Furthermore, we must put him on notice that his past victories over us are going to cost him dearly.

God's power is your power. Do not hesitate to use it on Satan and his demon hoard. You have nothing to fear, for you know that ". . . greater is He that is in you than he that is in the world" (1 John 4:4)! **God has given you the power and authority to take back everything the devil has stolen from you.**

Key #2 — The Law of Retribution

Once you understand it, **the Law of Retribution will become a powerful weapon in your hand.** It will show you your right to reclaim what the thief has stolen from you. Let's now look at these important scriptures in God's Word.

> If a man shall steal an ox, or a sheep, and kill it, or sell it; he shall restore five oxen for an ox, and four sheep for a sheep.
>
> If a thief be found breaking up, and be smitten that he die, there shall no blood be shed for him.
>
> . . . for he should make full restitution; if he have nothing, then he shall be sold for his theft.
>
> If the theft be certainly found in his hand alive, whether it be ox, or ass, or sheep; he shall restore double.
>
> If a man shall cause a field or vineyard to be eaten, and shall put in his beast, and shall feed in another man's field; of the best of his own field, and of the best of his own vineyard, shall he make restitution.
>
> If fire break out, and catch in thorns, so that the stacks of corn, or the standing corn, or the field, be consumed therewith; he that kindled the fire shall surely make restitution.
>
> If a man shall deliver unto his neighbor money or stuff to keep, and it be stolen out of the man's house; if the thief be found, let him pay double.
>
> If the thief be not found, then the master of the house shall be brought unto the judges, to see whether he have put his hand unto his neighbor's goods.
>
> For all manner of trespass [embezzlement], whether it be for ox, for ass, for sheep, for raiment, or for any manner of lost thing, which another challengeth to be his, the cause of both

> **parties shall come before the judges; and whom
> the judges shall condemn, he shall pay double
> unto his neighbor.**
> **Exodus 22:1-9**

It is absolutely necessary to understand these key verses. In them you will find God's detailed instructions about taking back stolen property. I have purposely placed them here in their entirety so that you can absorb them into your thinking process. Take an extra moment and mark them in your own Bible. Be sure to read them often so that they will go deep into your subconscious mind.

Even as I write I can imagine that you might be saying, "Brother John, why are you using such an old passage of Scripture? Doesn't the Old Testament pertain to Moses and the ancient people of the Bible? How can the Law of Retribution possibly apply to my present situation? I don't even own a vineyard, and the city where I live won't allow me to keep sheep in my backyard."

Please hear this carefully. The Lord never changes.

> **. . . Till heaven and earth pass, one jot or
> one tittle shall in no wise pass from the law, till
> all be fulfilled.**
> **Matthew 5:18**

Remember, the New Testament states clearly that we are to use the Old Testament for our instruction.

> **Now these things befell them . . . [as an
> example . . . to us]; they were written to . . . fit us
> for right action by good instruction. . . .**
> **1 Corinthians 10:11, Amplified**

As long as any of your possessions remain in the hands of the thief, these restitution verses will help you get them back. Read them over and over again. They were powerful when they were first written, and they are just as powerful today.

The World System Has Strange Ways

Some of the wording in God's Law of Retribution may sound strange to you in these modern times. The reason is that we live in a society where it is often against the law to defend your own property. The situation has become so ridiculous in some places, that if you hurt a thief while he is robbing your house, there is a good chance you will be held responsible for his medical expenses. He may even be able to sue you in a court of law. In most cases the modern court system seeks no repayment for damages victims suffer. Restitution is a thing of the past.

Please don't despair! I am not being negative. If the devil has victimized you, a higher court than the court of this world is available to you. God's court will sympathetically hear your appeal. **The powerful truth in this book will show you how to subpoena the devil and file an indictment against him in God's court.** If you do it right, it will bring a verdict of "guilty as charged." Remember this. **When God declares Satan guilty, he will have to pay you back everything he has stolen and more.**

Child of God, I believe you are beginning to feel new hope spring up inside. You are beginning to learn about Satan's method of operation. You now hold two life-changing keys in your hand. You know you can walk in the very power of God, and you know that God's Law of Retribution provides restitution. By the time you finish this book, you will know how to use these powerful keys to reclaim your stolen property.

3

The Powder-Puff Lion

I want to start this chapter by challenging a traditional concept. The Bible does not say Satan is a roaring lion. Satan would like for you to believe he is. However, that tradition simply is not the truth. Notice carefully that the Word of God actually says he goes about **as** a roaring lion.

> **Be sober, be vigilant; because your adversary the devil, AS a roaring lion, walketh about, seeking whom he may devour.**
> **1 Peter 5:8**

One of the primary goals of the devil is to cause you to believe he is a big and powerful lion. Through tricks and deception, he creates false images of his power.

Even as I write this, I can hear some of you say, "Brother John, don't tell me the devil isn't strong, for he has literally turned my life upside down. He has taken many of my prized possessions. He's destroyed my finances, led my children into sin, and taken the very joy of my salvation away from me. How can you possibly say he doesn't have any great power left?"

The Garden Snake Is Now a Dragon

Please do not misunderstand me. I am not advising you to turn your back and tell the devil to take his best shot. However, notice something strange. The garden snake of Genesis 3 turns into a dragon by the time we get to the Book of Revelation.

My, how big and fierce he seems to have become! How in the world did he grow so much? The truth is, someone has been feeding him! As strange as it may seem, **the saints of God give the devil most of the power he now possesses.** They do this by the words of their mouths. Remember, God says His children will have whatsoever they say.

> **For verily I say unto you, That whosoever shall say unto this mountain, Be thou removed, and be thou cast into the sea; and shall not doubt in his heart, but shall believe that those things which he saith shall come to pass; HE SHALL HAVE WHATSOEVER HE SAITH.**
> **Mark 11:23**

Without meaning to do so, the saints have poured a constant stream of power into the devil's hands over the last two thousand years. They have generated this power with words they have ignorantly spoken. This unintentional re-arming of the enemy has given him the ability to do some real damage.

Don't let these words alarm you. Even with this infusion of power, the Word of God says you can easily put your foot on Satan's head and hold him down.

> **And the God of peace shall bruise Satan under your feet shortly. . . .**
> **Romans 16:20**

Yes, you will be able to hold him in check if you will just **believe what God's Word says about your power** instead of what misinformed people say about the devil's power.

The Big Trick

The devil has pulled a big trick on the Church. Somehow he has caused Bible teachers to make a serious mistake in the way they teach the following verse of Scripture.

> **The thief cometh not, but for to steal, and to kill, and to destroy....**
> **John 10:10**

It is ironic, but the same teachers who attempt to stop the devil's work are actually building him up and giving him new power. They do so by teaching that the thief of John 10:10 is the devil. Let me quickly say that if the thief of this verse is the devil, then he does have the power to steal, kill, and destroy, and everything you will read in this book is wrong. However, it is clear from the context of this verse that John 10:10 does not even mention the devil.

When we speak of Satan as having the power to steal, we actually give him the power (or authority) to steal from us. If we speak of his power to kill, we give him the power he needs to take our very lives. As soon as we say he has the power to destroy, all of our belongings become subject to destruction.

How can all this possibly be? It is simple. **The power over life and death lives in the words of our mouth.** We can transfer this power to the devil in the words we speak about him.

> Death and life are in the power of the
> tongue. . . .
> #### Proverbs 18:21

When you read John 10:10 in its correct biblical context, the meaning is different from the traditional explanation. The first thing that becomes clear is that it speaks about hireling shepherds, those who come into the sheepfold with wrong motives. Jesus is warning us that these hireling teachers, prophets, and pastors cause danger and loss to the sheep.

Upon close observation, we can find the devil in this parable. He is the wolf of verse 12. The hireling shepherds are supposed to be watching out for the wolf (devil). Notice how quickly they flee the scene when he appears.

I can state without hesitation that John 10:10 does not depict the devil as the thief. Satan is none other than the wolf we see in verse 12.

Satan As a Thief

In one place Scripture does refer to Satan as a thief. The Bible tells us the only thing he can steal from us is the Word of God. However, I must once again emphasize that he can do this only if we let him.

> When any one heareth the word of the
> kingdom, and understandeth it not, then cometh
> the wicked one, and catcheth away that which
> was sown in his heart. This is he which received
> seed by the way side.
> #### Matthew 13:19

Please don't minimize the results of allowing him to steal the Word from you. This type of theft would make you weak, and then it would be easy for him to take the rest of your belongings. However, be careful about the concept of the thief in the Bible. Strange as it may seem, Scripture even uses it to describe our Lord. The Word plainly teaches that He will come ". . . as a thief in the night" (1 Thessalonians 5:2; 2 Peter 3:10).

Satan Had the Power of Death

One of the reasons the Church experiences so many untimely deaths is that the saints believe John 10:10 is a description of Satan's unlimited power to kill, steal, and destroy. If only we would spend more time teaching the saints about the power God has given to them, how quickly the devil's power would fade.

> **Behold, I GIVE UNTO YOU POWER to tread on serpents and scorpions, and OVER ALL THE POWER OF THE ENEMY: and nothing shall by any means hurt you.**
> **Luke 10:19**

The following verse is proof positive that John 10:10 is not speaking of any power Satan now possesses.

> **Forasmuch then as the children are partakers of flesh and blood, he also himself likewise took part of the same; that through death he might destroy him that HAD the power of death, that is, the devil.**
> **Hebrews 2:14**

Pay close attention to what this verse is actually saying to you. It says **God has taken the power of death from Satan.** It says plainly that he *used* to have the power of death. However, since the death, burial, and resurrection of Jesus Christ, he no longer has that power. Jesus has taken it away from him.

When the children of God learn just how severely God has limited the power of the devil, we will force him to take up permanent residence under our feet.

Only Six Ways to Die

Satan does not have the power to take your life. As far as I have been able to find, there are only six ways for a human being to die.

1. You can die by your own hand.

2. You can die by the hand of another human.

3. You can die from fearing death (Job 3:25).

4. You can die when you break natural laws (such as the law of gravity, aerodynamics, etc.).

5. You can die by being overcome by the aging process.

6. You can die as a result of sickness or disease.

Again I must say that in our day, the devil operates primarily in the power we have given him with our words. Remember, if you believe Satan can kill you, he will. If you believe he can rob you, he will. If you believe he has power to destroy you, he will.

Don't Kick a Dead Dog

When the children of God speak about the devil's power, it is just like kicking a dead dog. Kick a dead dog, and it will move. However, it moves only through the power it receives from the kick. It isn't the power of the dead dog that moves it; it's the power of the one who kicked it.

Satan is like a dead dog. He is defeated and powerless. However, when you speak that he has power over you, your words energize him, and he is able to move against you. He actually absorbs the power of your words and turns it against you.

In my younger days, I wasted much of my energy by battling with the devil because I didn't realize my power over him. I used to get in big fights with him. I would literally fight with his demons on the church platform. I would fight them in the homes of my congregation, and even out in the streets of our city. Then God showed me a better way. God showed me how to **use His power against the devil** instead of allowing the devil to use my power against me. Here's an illustration of that better way.

One Sunday a woman escorted her son who was about twenty-five years old, down the aisle of my church. When they got in front of me, the young man started slobbering and acting like a mad dog. Instead of openly rebuking the demon, I quickly shut off my microphone and looked squarely into his dazed eyes. Then with the authority of Jesus Christ Himself, I commanded, "In the name of Jesus, shut your mouth, you foul devil! Come out of him, and don't say a single word!" It took only a few words in the name of Jesus, and immediately the young man was calmed and the demon was gone.

As soon as you put your foot down in the name of Jesus, the devil cannot continue with his plan. Just stop energizing him with your words about his strength, and start rebuking him with God's Word about your strength over him.

Saint of God, wake up! **Jesus has given the devil a knock-out punch!** Drop that defeated mentality you picked up by speaking of how powerful the devil is. Move up to the overcoming mentality and confess how much power you have over the devil.

Satan Has Been Crushed

Let's look at still another example from God's Word of just how defeated Satan really is.

> **And when [the Holy Ghost] is come, he will reprove [convince] the world of sin, and of righteousness, and of judgment:**
> **Of judgment, because THE PRINCE OF THIS WORLD IS JUDGED.**
> **John 16:8,11**

Any good Greek dictionary will tell you that the word translated *judged* actually means "to separate or put asunder." To *put asunder* literally means "to break into pieces." That is not some vague definition of the word. It is the first and primary definition.

Jesus says the Holy Ghost has come to convince us that **Satan is broken into pieces.** Notice the great controversy that exists. While the Holy Spirit is telling us that Satan is defeated, literally broken into little pieces, well-meaning Bible teachers are telling us that the devil is alive and well, going about killing, stealing, and destroying.

If you read from John 16:11 to the end of the Bible, you will never again find a word about the devil's judgment. That is, until you read of an angel with a big chain and a set of keys in one hand putting him into the bottomless pit. Notice that it takes only one angel, and he does it with only one, free hand (Revelation 20:1-3).

There is just no better way to put it. **The devil is a defeated foe!** He's destroyed! He's all washed up! The Word of God says he's broken into pieces! Jesus has so thoroughly defeated him that it takes only one angel, using one hand, to throw him into the bottomless pit.

How in the world have we allowed ourselves to believe that this poor, pathetic has-been can rise up against us with any power at all? As soon as the Church sees the devil as he really is, we can immediately storm the strongholds of hell and take the world for Jesus!

I can hear someone say, "Brother John, if that's true, why do I still feel as if the devil has a powerful hold on me?"

The reason is simple. It is deception. Remember, the devil operates in the power of lying signs and fake wonders. You have the power to cast down any of these ideas he might try to place in your mind.

> (For the weapons of our warfare are not carnal, but mighty through God to the pulling down of strong holds;)
> CASTING DOWN IMAGINATIONS, and every high thing that exalteth itself against the knowledge of God, and bringing into captivity every thought to the obedience of Christ.
> 2 Corinthians 10:4,5

It is time for you to realize that the devil has no real power over you.

> Forasmuch then as the children are partakers of flesh and blood, he also himself

> likewise took part of the same; that through death he might DESTROY HIM THAT HAD THE POWER of death, that is, the devil.
> **Hebrews 2:14**

The word *destroy* is translated several ways in the New Testament. It is translated *without effect, made void, made of no effect,* and *abolish.* If the truth were known and every Christian walked in it, the devil would immediately have to go into intensive care. Hey, he is in really bad condition! The power he once had (past tense) is gone forever. Jesus was sent to destroy all of his works, and He did!

> . . . For this purpose the Son of God was manifested, that he might destroy the works of the devil.
> **1 John 3:8**

The Greek word translated here as *destroy* is *luo. Strong's Concordance* says it means "to loosen, . . . break up, . . . unloose, melt, put off." Do you understand what you are reading? **The devil has already been defeated!**

Some Need a Strong Devil

Let's get to the root of the problem. Perhaps you still struggle with accepting the devil's defeat because you are more comfortable with a strong devil. It may make you feel better if you can just blame everything on him.

No wonder we aren't ruling and reigning on earth! The Church is eager to hear preaching about the gospel of the King (salvation), but most Christians never hear much preaching about the gospel of the Kingdom (dominion).

Isn't it time we all laid hold on this truth? The primary thrust of our outreach must no longer be only getting people saved. We must begin to focus people's attention on their true heritage. We must help them grow up into the ". . . measure of the stature of the fullness of Christ" (Ephesians 4:13). This present generation of saints is an army of babies. We must now teach them the strong meat of the Word of God and help them grow up into an army of mature sons of God.

The Church has accepted the deception of Satan long enough. **It is time to reclaim everything that liar has stolen.** Let's walk in the full rights we have as sons and daughters of God!

Now that you know he is not the roaring lion he wants everyone to think he is, let's examine the three most common lies people tend to believe about the devil.

4

Satan Exposed and Deposed

By now I suppose you are beginning to think I have something against the devil. You are right. God has shown me that the devil is a bully. I am convinced he has ruled over Christians too long! It is high time the saints of God recognize he has no power compared to the power God has given us. We must expose him for the liar he is.

God's Word plainly tells us Satan is a defeated enemy. Yet people still believe so many lies about his power.

It is important to understand the three major lies folks most commonly believe about the devil. Your ability to recognize them will greatly reduce his power over you.

Lie #1: The Hollywood Hype

A few years ago, the entertainment industry made a decision to produce movies that glorify the devil's power. One movie that comes to mind was titled *Rosemary's Baby*. It portrayed Satan's power as the ultimate power. It showed humans to be virtually helpless against him. Because of the great earning power of *Rosemary's Baby*, Hollywood began to mass-produce many other movies like it with the hope that they, too, would make a fast profit.

One of the more popular follow-up movies was *The Exorcist.* Clever publicity agents associated its production with stories of mysterious things that supposedly took place. They made out every accident, sickness, or broken prop to be a manifestation of the devil. They erroneously warned prospective viewers to beware of the mystical dangers that might befall them if they watched the movie. At one point the hype was so high that theaters banned people with pacemakers from seeing it. With the aid of this publicity blitz, millions of Americans rushed into movie theaters to watch the devil do terrible things to people who were powerless to oppose him.

Over the years, Hollywood has continued to produce movies with this same false theme of the devil's unlimited power.

Hollywood Versus the Holy Word

One of the major problems the Church faces is that much of their knowledge about Satan and his power has come from Hollywood instead of the Holy Word. As movies showed the devil waging war with puny priests and wimpy preachers, Hollywood led people to believe God's power was inferior to the devil's. Tinsel Town tried to teach an entire generation of Christians that Satan can make them do whatever he wants them to do, and they are powerless to stop him.

Of course, the one who has benefited the most from this deception is Satan himself. Without realizing it, **many in the Church have subconsciously submitted themselves to believing Hollywood's impression of Satan.**

Deception Can Be Powerful

After hearing me teach that the devil is a defeated foe, a Christian brother told me the following story: "Brother John, a couple called upon my wife and me to pray for their little girl. The parents told us she was the victim of some severe demonic activity. They felt we had the anointing to rebuke the demon and see the child set free.

"In preparation, we fasted and prayed for a period of time. When the appointed day arrived, we were anxiously looking forward to serving notice on the devil. We eagerly awaited the opportunity to tell him his days of tormenting the child were over. However, as we were leaving our house, I noticed a strange thing going on in my mind. I was seeing vivid images of a child foaming at the mouth. I began to imagine her hurling knives at me through the power of her mind. I pictured her throwing me around the room with the strength of ten men. I literally saw her tossing us both out the door.

"While these thoughts were going through my mind, I suddenly remembered what you had taught us. 'One of the primary powers Satan has is deception.' Instantly I realized that despite my strong understanding of the Word, the casual viewing of some Hollywood movies had allowed the devil to influence my thinking process. **I was subconsciously accepting what Hollywood had so vividly shown me about Satan.**

"As soon as I realized the deception taking place, I cast down the evil imagination and went boldly forth in faith. My wife and I arrived at the girl's house, and just as the Bible promises, in the name of Jesus the victory came quickly. **God totally delivered the little girl!**"

See what the devil is doing? He is trying to get you subconsciously to accept Hollywood instead of the Holy Word. Don't allow his evil imaginations to enter your mind. Just remember, **the devil has no power over you except what you give him.**

> **Behold, I give unto you power to tread on serpents and scorpions, and over all the power of the enemy: and NOTHING SHALL BY ANY MEANS HURT YOU.**
> **Luke 10:19**

There is no possible way that Satan can cause a knife to come off a table and stab you. If he moves the knife, he must have help. Someone who gives his or her power over to the devil must control the knife, or Satan cannot move it.

Please believe the Word of God. By himself, the devil can't harm anyone. He can't do it alone. He must deceive someone into doing it for him.

Now here is a bold statement. Without the help of a willing human, the devil can't even make a feather move. He is powerless.

Lie #2: It's Just for Fun

Most Christians believe that if they had been the ones in the Garden of Eden, Satan would never have convinced them to eat of the forbidden fruit. They think they would have been too clever for the devil to trick them. Just think for a moment. Haven't you ever taken Satan's bait without even realizing it? Before you answer, you had better read the following six questions.

1. Have you ever read the horoscope column in the newspaper, just for fun?

2. Have you ever stopped in your tracks to avoid having a black cat cross your path? You know it's just a harmless superstition.

3. Have you ever thrown salt over your shoulder, just to make sure?

4. Have you ever hesitated before walking under a ladder, even though you know nothing would happen?

5. Do you allow your children to dress up as little devils or goblins at Halloween? After all, it's harmless fun.

6. Have you ever gone to a fortune teller, or played with an Ouija board? It's nothing serious. It's just for kicks.

If you answered no to all the above questions, congratulations! Let me say you are an exceptional person. If you answered yes to any of the above questions, it is time for you to serve notice on Satan. **Each of these are foolish and dangerous activities** that are nothing more than cleverly disguised traps.

> **There shall not be found among you any one that maketh his son or his daughter to pass through the fire, or that useth divination [fortune tellers], or an observer of times, or an enchanter, or a witch,**
> **Or a charmer, or a consulter with familiar spirits, or a wizard, or a necromancer.**
> **For all that do these things are an abomination unto the Lord ....**
> **Deuteronomy 18:10-12**

Watch out for superstitions and occult games, for they most certainly are not just for fun. They are deadly serious and are for no other reason than to trap people.

Lie #3: You Can Always Spot Evil

Many of God's children tend to become overconfident in their walk with the Lord. They come into a false sense of security, thinking no one will ever be able to deceive them. They think they will always be able to spot evil. However, this attitude is contrary to sound scriptural teaching.

> ... they shall deceive the very elect.
> **Matthew 24:24**

I once heard a girl testify that a Sunday school teacher led her into witchcraft. Satanically-inspired music lures many other young people from biblical Christianity. There are also so-called ministries that have developed a form of godliness, but demons actually control their leaders. (Jim Jones was one example.) The Apostle Paul was careful to warn us of such things.

> But I fear, lest by any means, as the serpent beguiled Eve through his subtilty, so your minds should be corrupted from the simplicity that is in Christ.
> For such are false apostles, deceitful workers, transforming themselves into the apostles of Christ.
> And no marvel; for Satan himself is transformed into an angel of light.
> Therefore, it is no great thing if his ministers also be transformed as the ministers of righteousness. ...
> **2 Corinthians 11:3,13-15**

Paul thought it necessary to warn the early church to be on guard against Satan's ministers disguised as God's messengers. How much more vigilant should we be in today's deceptive society? Jesus Himself warns us to watch out for deceivers.

> **. . . TAKE HEED THAT NO MAN DECEIVE YOU.**
> **For many shall come in my name, saying, I am Christ, and shall deceive many.**
> **Matthew 24:4,5**

Once again let me make it clear. One of the primary powers of Satan is deception. He wants you to accept the Hollywood hype and go along with the astrology and the fortune teller just for fun. He wants you to think he is totally different from how God says he is. I hope you know better than that. If you don't, he'll snag you for sure.

Don't let that happen! Remember, we are kings and priests. Jesus says we are light. We should never allow darkness to overcome light. We have a guarantee from God that **Satan cannot win if we walk in the fullness of the power God has given us.**

Now that I have exposed him for you, it's time to pull down the strongholds the devil has built against you. Don't allow him to deceive you any longer.

You are now ready to learn the four important steps you must take to reclaim your stolen property.

5

Step One:

Recognize Your Heritage

For many years I believed I was winning my war with Satan if the scoreboard read "John−51, Satan−49." However, that's not the way God envisions the score. He has made us more than conquerors (Romans 8:37). He wants us always to triumph. That means **we are supposed to win every time.**

> **Now thanks be unto God, which ALWAYS CAUSETH US TO TRIUMPH in Christ. . . .**
> **2 Corinthians 2:14**

As long as he is winning anything in your life, Satan is moving against God's will for you. God created you to be the winner.

Jesus Took His Weapons

The Bible plainly states that Jesus disarmed Satan and all his demon hoards.

> **[God] disarmed the principalities and powers that were ranged against us and made a bold display and public example of them, in triumphing over them in Him and in it [the cross].**
> **Colossians 2:15, Amplified**

Remember, the Word of God says we are always supposed to triumph, not just 51 percent of the time, not even 85 percent of the time, but always.

How much easier this sounds when we realize Satan has no weapon that will work against us.

> **No weapon that is formed against thee shall prosper; and every tongue that shall arise against thee in judgment thou shalt condemn. . . .**
> **Isaiah 54:17**

You Have a Part in the Battle

Please notice that this passage doesn't say *God* will condemn the tongues that rise up against you. It says *you* will condemn them. Misinformed teachers have been telling the Body of Christ that God will handle everything for them. God has no intention of fighting our battles for us. He has given us overcoming power to use on the enemy. Hear it again. God always causes *us* to triumph. **God expects us to take the offensive against the enemy and drive him out of his strongholds.**

Don't feel bad if you have had this teaching all backwards. It is common to find God's people waiting for God to fight their battles for them. Moses made this same mistake. He told the children of Israel to stand still and watch God fight for them.

> **And Moses said unto the people, Fear ye not, stand still, and see the salvation of the Lord, which he will show to you today: for the Egyptians whom ye have seen to day, ye shall see them again no more for ever.**
> **The Lord shall fight for you, and ye shall hold your peace.**
> **Exodus 14:13,14**

Hear the surprising way God reacted to the pious-sounding words of Moses.

> . . . WHEREFORE CRIEST THOU UNTO ME? speak unto the children of Israel, that they go forward:
> But lift thou up thy rod, and stretch out thine hand over the sea, AND [YOU] DIVIDE IT: and the children of Israel shall go on dry ground through the midst of the sea.
> Exodus 14:15,16

Notice that the children of Israel had a part to play in the victory over the Egyptians. God told Moses to instruct Israel to move forward in faith. Then He told Moses to divide the sea himself.

If you are going to have victory with God, you will have to participate in the battle. You will have to fight the good fight of faith. You will have to put your foot down on the devil's head.

Remember that your victory over him is not supposed to be a once-in-a-while event. God sees you winning every battle, every time. He sees you as instant in season and out of season (2 Timothy 4:2). The Word clearly says **the constant state of victory is your God-given heritage.** It is your birthright.

> . . . we are more than conquerors through him that loved us.
> Romans 8:37

God envisions you speaking forth His Word and treading down every enemy that opposes His will.

> Let the high praises of God be in their mouth, and a twoedged sword in their hand;

To execute vengeance upon the heathen, and punishments upon the people;

To bind their kings with chains, and their nobles with fetters of iron;

To execute upon them the judgment written: THIS HONOR HAVE ALL HIS SAINTS. Praise ye the Lord.

Psalm 149:6-9

Too often I hear misinformed Christians say, "I just know the Lord is going to take care of my financial problems for me." "The Lord will take care of my backsliding wife." "The Lord will see about my child who is on drugs." How full of faith these words sound! However, when the Lord doesn't take care of the situation, when the evil day comes and goes and nothing improves, these same folks immediately try to patch up their misconceptions by saying, "Well, I guess God was trying to teach me a lesson."

Nonsense! When we do not pull down the evil thoughts and strongholds of the devil, when we just leave it all up to God, then our ignorance gives occasion to the enemy. We are not supposed to be basket cases left in God's care. **We are to be actively involved with God in the business of the Kingdom.** One of the primary works in the Kingdom is to cast down and destroy all the works of the devil.

Wake up! God is your Father, and He is a good one! Good fathers don't teach their children by putting them through trials and tribulations. Good fathers teach obedient children by their words. He is teaching you by His Word so that **you can rise up and become the strong warrior God envisions you to be,** a warrior who will walk in all the authority He has given you. It is your heritage to be an overcomer.

> **For whatsoever is born of God overcometh the world: and this is the victory that overcometh the world, even our faith.**
> **1 John 5:4**

Hey, these verses are talking about a sure thing! God doesn't say you *might* overcome the world. He doesn't say you *may* overcome the world. God doesn't even say you will overcome the world *most of the time.* He boldly says you overcome the world, period. It's the end of the statement. **God expects you to win every time.**

Authority Outranks Ability

God has given you total power over the devil.

> **Behold, I give unto you power to tread on serpents and scorpions, and over all the power of the enemy: and nothing shall by any means hurt you.**
> **Luke 10:19**

The first word in this verse that is translated *power* is the Greek word *exousia.* It means "delegated power" or better said, "authority." The second word translated *power* is the Greek word *dunamis.* It means "ability." So notice carefully what God is actually saying. "I give you authority over all the ability of the devil."

Are you getting ahold of all of this? **You have total authority over all the ability of the enemy.** Remember, ". . . nothing shall by any means hurt you" (Luke 10:19).

It is possible you have never heard anything like this before. You may not even like the sound of it. However, I am duty bound as a man of God to put the truth before you. The Bible literally says nothing shall hurt you. It also says you have total power (authority) over the devil. You never have to lose again. You can *always* conquer and *always* triumph in *all* things.

Let's just go ahead and admit it. Satan has deceived all of us at one time or another. He has somehow tricked each of us into thinking God's Word doesn't mean exactly what it says. This, and this alone, is the reason we have not manifested the overcoming lifestyle spoken of in the Scriptures.

Please hear these words. God doesn't want the Church to spend another two thousand years making excuses. He wants us to believe Him instead of believing traditions and theologies. **It is time to stop explaining away the Word of God.** We must simply start believing it, declaring it, and best of all, manifesting it. Only then will the saints be able to manifest the greater works Jesus promised we would. Only then will we be able to do spiritual warfare in God's pure power.

> **For though we walk in the flesh, we do not war after the flesh:**
> **(For the weapons of our warfare are not carnal, but mighty through God to the pulling down of strong holds).**
> **2 Corinthians 10:3,4**

When the deceptive attacks of Satan come against us, too often we try to defend ourselves with carnal weapons. When we do, we always end up as the rest of the world does. You know how it works with them. When the devil says it's headache time, they simply obey and have a headache. When you operate with the world's weapons, you cannot help but end up with the world's results. You end up with whatever undesirable thing the devil can trick you into receiving.

Exercise Your Faith

I know you now realize it's time to rise up into the supernatural realm and take a firm hold on the heritage Jesus has purchased for you. Go ahead. Reach out and take it. As soon as you do, you will rise above the realm where the world chooses to live. You will immediately begin to feel God's power. It will help you reclaim all those things Satan has stolen.

Begin to exercise your faith. Break down the strongholds the devil has placed on your mind. Start with those things you find to be the easiest to handle. Remember, your faith doesn't start out eleven feet tall. It begins as a grain of mustard seed. As you exercise it, it will grow.

Begin applying your God-given rights. Start taking authority over the little things. When you have conquered them, go on to the next challenge. It won't take much of this new mentality until you find yourself walking in total victory. You will experience faith that is living and growing into dynamic new dimensions. You will actually marvel as you see how quickly the land of impossibility becomes one of possibility.

Ruling and Reigning Begins With Dominion

Down in your heart you already know that if you are going to rule and reign with Jesus, you must begin to take dominion over the moves Satan makes against you. You know if you cannot do a simple thing like getting rid of an evil thought, you will never be able to rule and reign with Christ. Only as you learn to bring your immediate circumstances under control, will you be able to create the atmosphere you need to stop the devil's violations against you.

God is gathering a people who will walk in their heritage, a people who will not just talk the Word, but will also walk the Word.

> **... faith, if it hath not works, is dead, being alone.**
>
> **James 2:17**

Jesus has purchased a victorious and triumphant life for you. It's available to you today. However, before you will be able to enjoy it fully, *you* must put the devil in his place. Remember, his place is under your feet (Romans 16:20). Once you realize God always causes you to triumph over Satan, you will quickly be able to reclaim everything he has stolen from you.

6

Step Two:
Accuse the Real Thief

If you are to receive restitution in the heavenly justice system, you must meet an important requirement. You must directly challenge the one who committed the wrongful act. I cannot emphasize this point too much. You cannot bring the wrong party into the celestial court system and expect to receive back any of your stolen property. **You must accuse the mastermind of the crime.**

Most of the time the children of God bring charges against the wrong party. They blame lawyers, financial consultants, business partners, deceptive salesmen, unsaved relatives, and so on. They continually blame flesh and blood beings for their losses.

Please hear me. If you insist on blaming your loss on human beings, there will never be any restoration for you. The Word of God clearly tells us we are not to fight our battles against flesh and blood (Hebrews 5:14).

You must remember that the devil is the engineer of every robbery. If you have suffered loss, it is because Satan has somehow gained the power to operate in another person's life. However, the human being involved is nothing more than an instrument the devil has used. As long as you keep blaming your circumstances on the people Satan uses, you will not be able to reclaim your stolen property.

Get ahold of the fact that it was the devil who ripped you off, no matter if he took your health, wealth, or loved ones. Fix it firmly in your mind. You are not supposed to wrestle with flesh and blood people.

> **For we wrestle not against flesh and blood,**
> **but against principalities, against powers,**
> **against the rulers of the darkness of this world,**
> **against spiritual wickedness in high places.**
> **Ephesians 6:12**

Your battle is with Satan and his demon hoards. You must focus on the devil as the instigator of every action taken against you and your possessions. He is the one you must accuse before the Father. Stop letting the activities of flesh and blood people distract you. Remember, God has divinely equipped you to fight your battles in heavenly places. You have your greatest power when you fight against Satan, for God has given you total power over him (Luke 10:19).

Remember, The Law of Retribution says **if you will put the cuffs on the real culprit, he will have to pay you at least double,** and possibly even as much as seven times the amount he stole.

Practice Makes Perfect

If you have been blaming people for your losses instead of blaming the devil, it may take a little while for you to learn to operate in this new mentality. However, the more you **practice confronting the true thief** in every robbery, the more quickly you will recover your stolen property.

> **But strong meat belongeth to them that are of full age [maturity], even those who by reason of use [practice] have their senses exercised to discern both good and evil.**
> **Hebrews 5:14**

When it speaks of full age, this verse is speaking of maturity. God is saying that exercising your God-given rights and powers speeds you to maturity. To put it into a commonly used saying, "practice makes perfect."

Let me give some examples from my own process of maturity. There came a time when I decided not to drink alcohol. I made this decision because I felt it was God's will for me. Now, after many years of not drinking, I don't even desire strong drink anymore. By habitually abstaining from alcohol, I have disciplined myself until I no longer desire it. The practice of not drinking has made it easy for me not to drink.

Many years ago I quit smoking cigarettes because I knew they were hurting my Christian testimony. I now travel extensively. No doubt I could lock myself up in a hotel room and have a smoke. I am sure no one would ever know I had done it. However, my body no longer wants a cigarette. The practice of not smoking has helped to bring a degree of perfection into my life. Now I no longer desire to smoke. That which was difficult when I was immature is now much easier since I have matured some.

In the same way, each time you practice accusing Satan, each time you choose to do battle with him instead of wrestling with flesh and blood, your skill in the Law of Retribution will increase. Constantly bringing the devil into God's courtroom will strengthen you and weaken him. **Each time you accuse Satan, you will become more**

skilled at getting your stolen property back, and the devil will become a bit more reluctant about stealing from you in the future.

7

Step Three:

Issue the Restraining Order

In the court system of the world, there is a legal document called "a restraining order." Its purpose is to stop the person it names from performing certain unwanted actions against another.

A common use of the restraining order is to prevent one person from doing harm to another person or his property. The restraining order legally forbids the person it names from entering the premises or coming near the property of the other person. It makes it possible for one person to bind the power of another.

This is also true in the heavenly court system. **God has provided a method whereby you can issue a restraining order against Satan.** It is fully enforceable and stops him cold in his attempts to harass or cause you loss. God's own Word tells us how to issue these binding orders against the devil.

> Verily I say unto you, WHATSOEVER YE SHALL BIND ON EARTH SHALL BE BOUND IN HEAVEN: and whatsoever ye shall loose on earth shall be loosed in heaven.
> Again I say unto you, That if two of you shall agree on earth as touching any thing that

they shall ask, it shall be done for them of my
Father which is in heaven.
Matthew 18:18-19

Yes, you have the God-given power to restrain Satan.
You can tie him up with strong cords. You can literally
bind him so that he can no longer take action against you.
Binding him works in your finances, job, business affairs,
personal life, health, and in any other area of your life he
has attacked.

Note carefully how God's Word puts it. The power of
your heavenly restraining order comes from a key
ingredient called "agreement."

. . . **IF TWO OF YOU SHALL AGREE on
earth as touching [pertaining to] any thing that
they shall ask, it shall be done for them of my
Father. . . .**
Matthew 18:19

Think back to the account in the Book of Exodus when
the Amalekites and the Israelites fought in the wilderness.
Moses stood on a hill with the rod of God in his hands. As
long as he held up his arms, Israel would win. However,
when he dropped his hands in fatigue, the enemy would
begin to overcome Israel.

The arms of Moses grew so weary he could no longer
hold them up. Then help came from Aaron and Hur, who
held up Moses' hands.

. . . **Aaron and Hur stayed up his hands, the
one on the one side, and the other on the other
side; and his hands were steady until the going
down of the sun.**
Exodus 17:12

Because Aaron and Hur stood in agreement with Moses, Israel had a quick victory.

In accomplishing your victory over Satan, you must realize the value of having someone stand in agreement with you. If Satan has robbed you of precious possessions, be it a child, treasure, relationship, or whatever, come quickly into agreement with someone whom you know has power over the devil. Together you will be able to bind Satan from any further attacks on your goods. Agree that the restraining order you form will quickly stop the devil from taking advantage of you. Then boldly begin to reclaim the thing he has taken. Pray in agreement that he immediately returns your goods and belongings.

Remember, **you cannot retrieve your stolen property unless you take strong action.** When the five kings in Genesis 14 took Lot and all of his goods, Abraham didn't go to retrieve them armed with only a willow switch. He took a strong force against them.

> **And when Abram heard that his brother was taken captive, he armed his trained servants, born in his own house, three hundred and eighteen, and pursued them unto Dan.**
> **And he divided himself against them, he and his servants, by night, and smote them, and pursued them unto Hobah, which is on the left hand of Damascus.**
> **And he brought back all the goods, and also brought again his brother Lot, and his goods, and the women also, and the people.**
> **Genesis 14:14-16**

When you go into the enemy's camp to retrieve your stolen property, be sure to go with strong agreement behind you. Come into agreement with one who fully understands what you are attempting to do. Remember, you are not just having a little prayer meeting. **You are serving a restraining order on the deceiver.** Be sure you go in with a mature saint. Then take hold of the ultimate weapon, the name of Jesus. You and your qualified partner must bind Satan in that strong name.

Please don't try to bind Satan just because I say to do it. Bind him because the Word of God tells you to do it. If you notice the following verse from our Lord's own mouth, you will see He believes binding the enemy to be the only way to repossess your goods.

> **No man can enter into a strong man's house, and spoil his goods, EXCEPT HE WILL FIRST BIND THE STRONG MAN; and then he will spoil his house.**
>
> **Mark 3:27**

I Will Help You

Before you can take back your goods, you must first restrain the strong man. Almost every day I go into the strong man's (devil's) house to bind him. I go with folks just like you. Together we speak strong words of agreement and faith. We have taken back much stolen property in this way.

If you wish me to join you in binding the strong man, I am ready to come into agreement with you. I will help you issue your restraining order on the devil. (Please see Chapter 11 for details.)

8

Step Four:
Make the Thief Return It
With Interest

God expects His children to earn interest on their money and goods. This principle is evident from Scripture. In the Book of Matthew, we see the master sternly rebuke a wicked servant for leaving his money dormant. He tells him the least he could have done was to place the money with the money changers so that he could have drawn interest.

> **His lord answered and said unto him, Thou wicked and slothful servant . . . .**
> **Thou oughtest therefore to have put my money to the exchangers, and then at my coming I should have received mine own with usury.**
> **Matthew 25:26,27**

God doesn't want you deprived of your goods without full reimbursement, plus interest.

Notice carefully that each of the robberies or losses mentioned in the Law of Retribution (Exodus 22:1-9) carries with it a heavy penalty. For each ox stolen, a man had to return five oxen. That amounts to 500 percent interest. Keep in mind that oxen were valuable in the economy of that time. An ox would be comparable to a farmer's tractor or a merchant's delivery van in our day. Almost everything would stop functioning for the Israelite who had an ox stolen. The theft would mean financial disaster.

If the thief couldn't pay the fine, he was sold into slavery. Then his victim would receive the money from the sale.

If a man's field burned due to negligence on the part of another, the guilty party was to give the best of his field to the person who had suffered the loss. Even if he did not deliberately cause the loss, he had to replace the field. Even if the burned crop was inferior or substandard, the negligent party had to replace it with the best he had.

If a thief stole money, he had to restore double the amount he took. The law demanded an increase of 100 percent.

By the time we come to the Book of Proverbs, the penalty is even harsher. There we read that **a thief must pay back seven times as much as he stole.** That amounts to a whopping 700 percent penalty for stealing money.

> **Men do not despise a thief, if he steal to satisfy his soul when he is hungry;**
> **But if he be found, HE SHALL RESTORE SEVENFOLD; he shall give all the substance of his house.**
>
> **Proverbs 6:30,31**

Let me give a brief explanation of the increase of the penalty from 100 percent in Exodus 22:7 to 700 percent in Proverbs 6:31. Much time had passed between these two verses. When Moses wrote the Book of Exodus, the Israelite population was primarily rural. Their ability to farm was the base of their existence. However, at the time Solomon wrote the Book of Proverbs, society had begun to move to the cities. Urban life made money much more important to daily survival. Therefore, as the value of money increased, the penalty for stealing it also increased.

File Your Claim in God's Court

Make no mistake about it. God operates his justice system much differently from the way the world does. The United States system of justice isn't interested nearly so much in restitution for the victim of a crime as it is in fair treatment of the criminal. Because of this attitude, **it is important to file your lawsuit in the courthouse of God,** for God will serve your best interest.

I encourage you to calculate how much the devil has stolen from you. When you have made this calculation, don't forget to add the interest he owes you. Just multiply the amount by seven. Then boldly proceed with your claim. (See Chapter 11 for details on how to file your lawsuit against the devil.)

9

God's Theft-Protection Policy

I have good news for you. Not only does He want you to reclaim your stolen property, but **God also has a special plan that can render your life burglar-proof.** The conditions of this spiritual theft-protection policy are clearly given to us in the Word of God.

> Put on the whole armor of God, that ye may be able to stand against the wiles of the devil.
>
> For we wrestle not against flesh and blood, but against principalities, against powers, against the rulers of the darkness of this world, against spiritual wickedness in high places.
>
> Wherefore take unto you the whole armor of God, that ye may be able to withstand in the evil day, and having done all, to stand.
>
> Stand therefore, having your loins girt about with truth, and having on the breastplate of righteousness;
>
> And your feet shod with the preparation of the gospel of peace;
>
> Above all, taking the shield of faith, wherewith ye shall be able to quench all the fiery darts of the wicked.
>
> And take the helmet of salvation, and the sword of the Spirit, which is the Word of God:
>
> Praying always with all prayer and supplication in the Spirit. . . .
>
> **Ephesians 6:11-18**

I hope you have figured out by now that you are in a spiritual war. Satan is the enemy. Either you bring him into containment, or he will bring you into containment. You will be able to overcome him if you use God's plan.

By yourself you are no match for Satan. He will deceive you and take everything from you. However, when you choose to walk in God's strength, **the devil is no match for you.** Notice God tells you to put on the whole armor, not just part of it, but all of it.

Think about this. If your house burned down because you built a bonfire in the living room, you would be foolish to expect your home insurance carrier to cover your losses. He would quickly tell you that your actions were not those of a rational person. He would say building a bonfire in your house is a foolish act. No court would instruct him to cover your losses if you had purposely caused them.

It works the same way with God. **If you arm yourself according to God's policy, you will be under complete protection.** If you don't, there will be no way to protect yourself from the devil's attacks.

Six Steps to Full Coverage

Notice the six things God says you must be doing in your life if you want to enjoy complete coverage under his protection.

1. You must wrap your loins with truth.

In the world system, men fight legal battles with lies, exaggerations, evasions, and cover-ups. The main job of an attorney is not centered around truth. It centers around the protection of his client, even if he has to suppress the truth.

In God's courtroom, truth prevails. Your attorney is the incarnation of truth. He is none other than the Lord Jesus Christ Himself.

> **. . . I am the way, the truth, and the life. . . .**
> **John 14:6**

Yes, the Bible tells us Jesus is our attorney.

> **. . . we have an advocate [attorney] with the**
> **Father, Jesus Christ the righteous.**
> **1 John 2:1**

Your spiritual theft-protection policy will demand you to be truthful. Disregarding the truth will cause you to forfeit the battle to the father of lies. If you do not deal in truth, you literally open the doors of your house and invite Satan in to take whatever he wants from you.

Truth is the foundation of God's theft-protection policy. Watch your words carefully. Keep yourself wrapped in the truth.

2. You must wear the breastplate of righteousness.

If you want protection from the devil, you must also stand before God in true righteousness. Don't get caught up in the false righteousness men try to create by their own works. We have no righteousness except what comes through faith in Jesus Christ.

> **But we are all as an unclean thing, and all**
> **our righteousnesses are as filthy rags. . . .**
> **Isaiah 64:6**

If there is hidden sin in your life, Satan will use it to overthrow you. Hidden sin makes it easy for him to take your goods. When you find sin in your life, go immediately to Jesus and ask for forgiveness. As soon as you do this, the devil loses his ability to steal from you.

> **If we confess our sins, he is faithful and just to forgive us our sins, and to cleanse us from all unrighteousness.**
>
> **1 John 1:9**

The more you stand in God's righteousness, the more quickly God can work. He says He can literally cut short the time it will take to do His work against Satan, if we have righteous lives for Him to work in and through.

> **For he will finish· the work, and cut it short in righteousness. . . .**
>
> **Romans 9:28**

3. You must cover your feet with the gospel of peace.

This requirement simply means you must always be about the business of telling the world about the Prince of Peace. You must be sharing the good news that Jesus lived, died, rose again, and is alive today at the right hand of the Father. Remember, Scripture looks upon your feet as the vehicle which carries the gospel message to others.

> **How beautiful upon the mountains are the feet of him that bringeth good tidings, that publisheth peace; that bringeth good tidings of good, that publisheth salvation; that saith unto Zion, Thy God reigneth!**
>
> **Isaiah 52:7**

Many Christians limit God's power in their lives by not going daily into the world with the message about the

Prince of Peace. Please remember, world evangelism is not optional. It's mandatory.

> ... Go ye into all the world, and preach the
> gospel to every creature.
> **Mark 16:15**

Child of God, He did not limit this command to the missionaries and evangelists. **God gave this command to everyone who claims Jesus as Lord and Savior.** He told us to tell everyone that Jesus is the Christ, the Savior of the world.

As your feet take you from one place to another, share the gospel of peace as you go. Each time you do, you will be fulfilling one of the conditions of your spiritual theft-protection policy.

4. You must carry the shield of faith.

Christians are doing so many religious works, things they sincerely believe are pleasing God. However, one basic ingredient must be present with every work we do for God if we are to please Him. That ingredient is faith!

> But without faith it is impossible to please
> him. ...
> **Hebrews 11:6**

Faith is crucial to your theft-protection plan. Not only is it "... the substance of things hoped for, ..." it is also the part of your armor that quenches the fiery darts of the devil. It is what makes you strong and the devil weak.

The Word of God clearly states it is our faith that overcomes the world.

> **For whatsoever is born of God overcometh the world: and THIS IS THE VICTORY THAT OVERCOMETH THE WORLD, EVEN OUR FAITH.**
>
> **1 John 5:4**

Because so many wonderful teachings on faith are available to Christians today, I will not spend time on this subject in this book. However, I do recommend that you regularly increase your understanding of it. **Faith is probably the most vital element of your Christian growth.** It is a key part of your theft-protection policy.

5. You must wear the helmet of salvation.

Salvation is more than just asking Jesus to forgive you of your sins. Salvation is a daily walk with Him. It is a lifestyle. It is a progressive walk out of the old nature into the divine nature. Wearing the helmet of salvation means constantly seeking to make the Lord's mind your mind.

> **Let this mind be in you, which was also in Christ Jesus.**
>
> **Philippians 2:5**

Football players wear helmets for a good reason. The helmet acts as a shock absorber. No matter how severe the impact of a tackle might be, the helmet protects the head. This protection allows the player to continue the contest without being disoriented each time his opponent blocks him.

In the same way, the helmet of salvation will protect your mind. Let there be no doubt about it. **When you meet Satan, it will be on the battlefield of your mind.** When he assaults you, his powerful blows could disorient you. However, if you know who you are in Christ, you will be able to go on to victory without being stunned and confused. This kind of progress will be possible only if you are wearing the helmet of salvation.

6. You must utilize the Word of God.

No true soldier would think of going into a battle unarmed. The enemy would delight in such a foolish move. Yet so many Christians try to wage spiritual warfare without properly using the main weapon God has given them. The Word of God is a mighty offensive weapon. It can cut down every deception and lie the enemy sends your way.

> **No weapon that is formed against thee shall prosper. . . .**
> **Isaiah 54:17**

Think about how seldom most Christians come into contact with the Word of God. Numerous children in every church congregation can easily recite the latest hamburger commercial, but they may have never memorized even one verse of Scripture. I know adults who can quote the stock market by the hour, yet they haven't committed any appreciable amount of Scripture to memory.

How will you ever fight a spiritual war if you don't even have a working knowledge of your weapon? Hamburger commercials will come and go. Stock market prices will rise and fall, but **the Word of God will never change.**

> **Heaven and earth shall pass away: but my words shall not pass away.**
> **Mark 13:31**

Satan cannot prevail against you if you are armed with the Word of God. Notice when I say "armed with the Word of God," I don't mean just having it tucked neatly under your arm. I mean faithfully committing it to your mind and understanding. The Word of God will always serve you if you know what it says.

> . . . the word of the Lord is tried: he is a buckler [defender, shield, protector] to all those that trust in him.
>
> **Psalm 18:30**

If we put on God's full suit of armor, He promises we will stand victorious in the evil day. With every part in place, we will easily win. God's theft-protection plan will work for those who work it.

> So use every piece of God's armor to resist the enemy whenever he attacks, and when it is all over, you will still be standing up.
>
> **Ephesians 6:13, TLB**

10

Who Is Behind Your Troubles

If there is a key thought in this book, it has to be this: **The devil is the mastermind behind every evil act that takes place on this earth.** The Bible abounds with evidence that he is the villain behind all the trouble. Whether it be sickness, disappointment, robbery, or what have you, the source of the problem is the same. It is the devil.

God Made a Good Universe

Things do not tend toward evil because God planned them that way. Evil is an unnatural intruder in God's creation. It came into the human race with the fall, not with the creation. The truth is, even Satan himself was perfect when God created him. God later found evil in him.

> Thou art the anointed cherub that covereth . . . .
> Thou wast perfect in thy ways from the day that thou wast created, till iniquity was found in thee.
> **Ezekiel 28:14,15**

Satan Caused the Fall

Who is guilty for the fall of man? The Book of Genesis gives us the answer to this question. Notice that Adam began by blaming Eve.

> **And the man said, The woman whom thou gavest to be with me, she gave me of the tree, and I did eat.**
>
> **Genesis 3:12**

However, it was Eve who put the blame where it belonged. She named Satan as the evil force behind the fall.

> **. . . And the woman said, The serpent beguiled me, and I did eat.**
>
> **Genesis 3:13**

Notice that as soon as Eve named the true thief, God immediately brought the Law of Retribution into action against Satan.

> **. . . Because thou hast done this, thou art cursed above all cattle . . . and dust shalt thou eat all the days of thy life:**
>
> **And I will put enmity between thee and the woman, and between thy seed and her seed; it shall bruise thy head, and thou shalt bruise his heel.**
>
> **Genesis 3:14,15**

As soon as she accused the true thief, swift judgment came. **Because Eve refused to wrestle with flesh and blood, God was able to bring speedy restoration.**

Satan Caused Job's Problems

Let's look at another biblical example. In the Book of Job we find the account of one of the greatest robberies that has ever taken place. Just look at the inventory of goods stolen from Job.

> . . . seven thousand sheep, and three thousand camels, and five hundred yoke of oxen, and five hundred she asses, and a very great household. . . .
>
> **Job 1:3**

From all across Job's vast empire the evil reports started pouring in. All of his oxen, donkeys, sheep, and camels were stolen. All his children died. All except three of his servants were slain. Job suffered tremendous loss in just one day. However, I want you to take careful notice of who received the blame for this theft in the first chapter of Job.

Verse 15 tells us that the Sabeans took the oxen and donkeys, and killed some of the servants. Verse 16 blames God for burning up the sheep and other servants. (I hope you grasp the significance of this accusation. Many people are still blaming God today when they suffer loss. Insurance policies commonly allow for so-called "acts of God," which they always interpret to be things destructive and harmful to man.)

Verse 17 accuses the Chaldeans of taking the camels and slaying still more servants. Verses 18 and 19 blame the wind for the deaths of the children. However, verses 6-12 show us clearly who was actually responsible for Job's loss. God spoke to Satan and said:

> . . . Behold, all that [Job] hath is in thy
> power. . . .
>
> **Job 1:12**

Scripture identifies the real thief to be Satan. He was the one who masterminded all the robberies and killings, for God gave everything in Job's life over to his power. The Sabeans didn't mastermind the losses. The Chaldeans weren't the culprits. The wind wasn't to blame. God, most assuredly, didn't cause them. It was none other than our old enemy, the devil!

Jesus Used This Principle

God has always recognized the true culprit. In the Book of Mark, we find that just prior to the crucifixion, Simon Peter tried to stop Jesus from going to Jerusalem. To the casual observer this attempt was nothing more than a devoted disciple's desire to keep his master from being killed. However, Jesus always walked with His spiritual eyes open. He knew Peter was receiving outside interference. Jesus immediately brought charges against the deceptive force behind Peter's seeming concern. Notice carefully whom Jesus accused.

> . . . Get thee behind me, Satan: for thou
> savorest not the things that be of God, but the
> things that be of men.
>
> **Mark 8:33**

Jesus understood that Peter was allowing the devil to use him. He knew Satan was the motivating force behind the rebuke Peter had given Him. As always, the devil was at the root of the problem.

There is nothing unusual about what I am describing to you. This scenario takes place every day in the courts of our land. When someone gets shot, the police don't file charges against the gun. The gun that did the shooting was only the instrument. The guilty party is the one who had control of the gun and pulled the trigger.

A Spiritual Problem

As you read the following scriptures, allow your mind to focus on a principle that will set you free. When you understand it, the real thief will have to make full restitution.

> And he was teaching in one of the synagogues on the sabbath.
>
> And, behold, there was a woman which had A SPIRIT OF INFIRMITY eighteen years, and was bowed together, and could in no wise lift up herself.
>
> And when Jesus saw her, he called her to him, and said unto her, Woman, thou art loosed from thine infirmity.
>
> And he laid his hands on her: and immediately she was made straight, and glorified God.
>
> And the ruler of the synagogue answered with indignation, because that Jesus had healed on the sabbath day, and said unto the people, There are six days in which men ought to work: in them therefore come and be healed, and not on the sabbath day.
>
> The Lord then answered him, and said, Thou hypocrite, doth not each one of you on the sabbath loose his ox or his ass from the stall, and lead him away to watering?
>
> And ought not this woman, being a daughter of Abraham, WHOM SATAN HATH BOUND, lo, these eighteen years, be loosed from this bond on the sabbath day?

> **And when he had said these things, all his adversaries were ashamed: and all the people rejoiced for all the glorious things that were done by him.**
>
> **Luke 13:10-17**

In this passage, we see a woman who was bowed over, unable to straighten up. The rulers thought she had a physical problem, one Jesus should not deal with on the Sabbath day. The rulers blamed her health, but Jesus saw what was really happening. Satan, not paralysis, not an irregular spine, but Satan, had bound the woman.

Notice that as soon as Jesus named the real culprit, two things happened. Joy came to the multitudes and shame to the adversary.

You see, the religious leaders of that day saw her as a sick woman. If they had tried to help her, they would have been wrestling with flesh and blood, for they saw only the physical problem.

Jesus saw her as a woman bound by the devil. **He saw a spiritual problem,** one that was fair game for the Sabbath. In naming the true thief, Jesus immediately brought the woman into full restitution and restored her body's mobility. Satan had robbed this woman for eighteen years. Then **on the day Jesus identified the true villain and took him to court, God set her free.**

Jesus always saw who the true culprit was. He immediately identified him, even among his own hand-picked disciples.

> **. . . Have not I chosen you twelve, and one of you is a devil?**
>
> **John 6:70**

Judas was a disciple from the beginning. He had personally witnessed many miracles. He even performed miracles.

> **And when he had called unto him his twelve disciples [Judas included], he gave them power against unclean spirits, to cast them out, and to heal all manner of sickness and all manner of disease.**
> **Matthew 10:1**

Yet even with this first-hand knowledge of our Lord, Judas allowed the enemy to motivate him. Jesus was never in the dark about the strange behavior of Judas. He knew full well that his unfaithfulness was the manifestation of a far greater problem. It was Satan at work.

Peter Received Restoration

Please notice that if Satan has deceived you, you are not permanently disqualified from serving God. Even after he denied the Lord three times in a row, Peter was later able to identify the devil at work in the lives of others. We have proof in the account of Ananias and Sapphira.

As you probably know, Ananias and Sapphira secretly devised a plot to gain prestige in the Body of Christ through deception. They had seen Barnabas gain approval from the people when he gave the Church all the money from the sale of a piece of property. They decided they would gain that same approval. However, Satan convinced them to do it at a reduced rate. The result of this deception was death.

Simon Peter immediately recognized the true culprit behind their deception. It was Satan himself. **Notice that he didn't hesitate to expose the devil's undercover tactics.**

> . . . Ananias, why hath Satan filled thine
> heart to lie. . . ?
>
> **Acts 5:3**

Paul Used This Principle

The Apostle Paul was always aware of who his true
enemy was. He openly stated men did not cause his
problems, but they came from a messenger that Satan sent.

> . . . there was given to me a thorn in the
> flesh, the messenger of Satan to buffet me. . . .
> **2 Corinthians 12:7**

This messenger buffeted Paul using a number of
people against him. These were false brothers, evil
magistrates, and various inquisitors. However, no matter
what form the opposition took, Paul always understood
they were only instruments Satan used. He always laid the
ax to the root of the problem. Notice whom he blamed for
his failure to visit Thessalonica.

> . . . we would have come unto you, even I
> Paul, once and again; but Satan hindered us.
> **1 Thessalonians 2:18**

When he suspected trouble among the Thessalonian
saints, Paul didn't wrestle with flesh and blood. He
immediately sent Timothy to find out where the devil had
attacked them.

> . . . lest by some means the tempter have
> tempted you.
> **1 Thessalonians 3:5**

Paul identified the root of the trouble that the widows
in the Church seemed to have caused.

> . . . they learn to be idle . . . speaking things
> which they ought not.
> . . . give none occasion to the adversary to
> speak reproachfully.
> For some are already turned aside after
> Satan.
>
> 1 Timothy 5:13-15

To sum it up, **the Bible lays the blame for the entire sin problem at Satan's feet.**

> He that committeth sin is of the devil; for
> the devil sinneth from the beginning. . . .
>
> 1 John 3:8

The devil is the root of sin. If you are ever going to put your life in order, you must realize that Satan is the real source of any problem. Just say it boldly. Accuse him out loud. "Satan, you are at the bottom of all my problems." As soon as you learn to accuse him, the doors of total restoration will begin to open. The things the devil has stolen from you will immediately begin to return.

Salvation Is the Beginning of Retribution

If you are not saved, get saved today. The number one way to start receiving the benefits of the Law of Retribution is by accepting Jesus as your Savior. When you change from serving the god of this world (Satan) to the God of the Word, restoration begins.

> Wherein in time past ye walked according to
> the course of this world, according to the prince
> of the power of the air, the spirit that now
> worketh in the children of disobedience.
> But God, who is rich in mercy, . . .
> . . . hath quickened us together with Christ,
> (by grace ye are saved;)

**And hath raised us up together, and made
us sit together in heavenly places in Christ Jesus.
Ephesians 2:2, 4-6**

After conversion, faithfully apply the principles in this book, and full restoration will be yours.

Remember, you must stop accusing men and circumstances.

**For we wrestle not against flesh and blood,
but against principalities, against powers,
against the rulers of the darkness of this world,
against spiritual wickedness in high places.
Ephesians 6:12**

Start accusing Satan, for he is the real thief. The Law of Retribution is real, and it is ready to go to work for you. God wants to help you reclaim everything the devil has ripped off. He is waiting for you to file your lawsuit.

Remember, the Word says that when you catch him, the thief must pay.

A Bold Confession

Say this out loud:

"Devil, I put you on notice. This is the last day you will steal from me. Your days of ripping me off are over. I now have advanced knowledge. This knowledge will knock you out and put me on top. It will put you under my feet and force you to give back to me everything you have ever stolen from me.

"Oh, yes. There is just one more thing, Mr. Devil. You will also have to pay me interest, seven times the amount you stole.

Get ready, for I am filing a lawsuit against you, and I am not filing it in your earthly court system. I am filing it in my God's heavenly courthouse."

11

Let Me Help You File Your Claim

"Brother John, your book has opened my eyes. I want to take back everything the devil has stolen from me."

"I feel better now that I know the truth, but I'm not going to feel really good until I get everything back, plus interest."

If these are your sincere feelings, I will commit myself to help you. Following this chapter, you will find a brief form. I call it "The Restoration Mandate and Restraining Order."

Prayerfully and carefully fill it out. Then quickly send it to me. I will personally hold it up before God and stand in agreement with you as we bring charges against the devil. I will then put it in a special place where my family and I will pray over it for at least thirty days. We will be specific in asking God for quick action on your request.

Please notice that I do not extend this offer of agreement lightly. **I know that when you and I agree together, we will generate great spiritual power.**

> Verily I say unto you, Whatsoever ye shall bind on earth shall be bound in heaven: and whatsoever ye shall loose on earth shall be loosed in heaven.
> Again I say unto you, That if two of you shall agree on earth as touching any thing that

**they shall ask, it shall be done for them of my
Father which is in heaven.**
Matthew 18:18,19

Please be as sincere in this as I am, for only in that way
will we force Satan to loose his grip from the things he has
stolen from you.

As soon as you receive your property back, please
write and give me all the details. All of us here at my
ministry headquarters are eager to hear about your victory
over the devil. We also want to know exactly how much
damage we have helped you to cause against the kingdom
of darkness.

Please fill out one of the restoration mandates that
follows. As you will notice, I have placed several of these
forms in your book. I hope you will be able to help others
take back the things the devil has stolen from them. I will
gladly join with anyone you recommend to our ministry,
for agreement in filing a Restoration Mandate and
Permanent Restraining Order.

The Restoration Mandate
and Permanent Restraining Order

Name_____

Address_____

City_____State_____Zip_____

Area Code and Phone Number (_____)_____

Hear me, Lord. Hear me, angels. Hear me, men. This day I am joining my faith with John Avanzini. We are coming in the name of Jesus, and we are demanding that the devil give up the following belongings of mine which he has stolen. (Use back of page if you need more space.)

1._____ 4._____

2._____ 5._____

3._____ 6._____

We make this order according to God's Law of Retribution from Exodus 22:1-9. We also demand he refund to me seven times the amount he has taken, according to Proverbs 6:30,31. We further come boldly and place on Satan a valid and enforceable restraining order.

Lord, both John Avanzini and I are fully clothed in the six pieces of armor you insist we wear if we want to win. We both agree to hold this request up to the Father. We have promised to do so in the strong name of Jesus.

Signature:_____**Date:**_____

Witnessed: *1)The Father 2)The Son 3)The Holy Ghost*

Brother John, while I know you have not asked me to give anything, my heart has been blessed by this book and I want to make a special love offering to your ministry. Enclosed you will find my gift of $_____.
Use it wherever you feel it will do the most good.

The Restoration Mandate and Permanent Restraining Order

Name_____

Address_____

City_____State_____Zip_____

Area Code and Phone Number (____)_____

Hear me, Lord. Hear me, angels. Hear me, men. This day I am joining my faith with John Avanzini. We are coming in the name of Jesus, and we are demanding that the devil give up the following belongings of mine which he has stolen. (Use back of page if you need more space.)

1._____4._____
2._____5._____
3._____6._____

We make this order according to God's Law of Retribution from Exodus 22:1-9. We also demand he refund to me seven times the amount he has taken, according to Proverbs 6:30,31. We further come boldly and place on Satan a valid and enforceable restraining order.

Lord, both John Avanzini and I are fully clothed in the six pieces of armor you insist we wear if we want to win. We both agree to hold this request up to the Father. We have promised to do so in the strong name of Jesus.

Signature:_____**Date:**_____

Witnessed: *1) The Father 2) The Son 3) The Holy Ghost*

Brother John, while I know you have not asked me to give anything, my heart has been blessed by this book and I want to make a special love offering to your ministry. Enclosed you will find my gift of $_____.
Use it wherever you feel it will do the most good.

The Restoration Mandate
and Permanent Restraining Order

Name_____

Address_____

City_____State_____Zip_____

Area Code and Phone Number (_____)_____

Hear me, Lord. Hear me, angels. Hear me, men. This day I am joining my faith with John Avanzini. We are coming in the name of Jesus, and we are demanding that the devil give up the following belongings of mine which he has stolen. (Use back of page if you need more space.)

1._____4._____

2._____5._____

3._____6._____

We make this order according to God's Law of Retribution from Exodus 22:1-9. We also demand he refund to me seven times the amount he has taken, according to Proverbs 6:30,31. We further come boldly and place on Satan a valid and enforceable restraining order.

Lord, both John Avanzini and I are fully clothed in the six pieces of armor you insist we wear if we want to win. We both agree to hold this request up to the Father. We have promised to do so in the strong name of Jesus.

Signature:_____**Date:**_____

Witnessed: *1) The Father 2) The Son 3) The Holy Ghost*

Brother John, while I know you have not asked me to give anything, my heart has been blessed by this book and I want to make a special love offering to your ministry. Enclosed you will find my gift of $_____.
Use it wherever you feel it will do the most good.

Books by John Avanzini

Always Abounding
Enter a new dimension of abundant living through a
plan from God's Word that cannot fail.   **$5.95**

Faith Extenders
Study how characters from the Bible caused their faith
to grow, and how you can use the same methods to
increase your faith today.   **$7.95**

Financial Excellence
This powerful treasury of wisdom is the result of many
years of Bible study and covers a number of dynamic
financial principles.   **$9.95**

Hundredfold
See clearly and thoroughly the scriptural laws of
seed-time and harvest, God's plan for your
increase.   **$7.95**

It's Not Working, Brother John!
If you've done all you know and still haven't received
God's promises, study these twenty-five things that
close the windows of heaven.   **$8.95**

John Avanzini Answers Your Questions
Find the answers to the twenty most-often-asked
questions about biblical economics.   **$6.95**

Powerful Principles of Increase
Find out how you can take the resources of this world to
establish God's Kingdom.   **$8.95**

Stolen Property Returned

Learn how to identify the real thief, take him to the heavenly courtroom, and recover what he has stolen.   **$5.95**

The Wealth of the World

Find help to prepare for your part in the great end-time harvest of souls and wealth.   **$6.95**

The Financial Freedom Series

War on Debt

Financial Freedom Series, Volume I — If you are caught in a web of debt, your situation is not hopeless. You can break the power of the spirit of debt.   **$7.95**

Rapid Debt-Reduction Strategies

Financial Freedom Series, Volume II — Learn practical ways to pay off all your debts — mortgage included — in record time.   **$12.95**

The Victory Book

Financial Freedom Series, Volume III — This workbook takes you step by step through The Master Plan for paying off every debt.   **$14.95**

Have a Good Report

Financial Freedom Series, Volume IV — Find out what your credit report says about you, and learn the steps that will help you correct negative information.   **$8.95**

**Complete both sides of this order form
and return it to HIS Publishing Co.
to receive a 10% discount
on your book order.**

Qty	Title	Cost	Total
	Always Abounding	5.95	
	Faith Extenders	7.95	
	Financial Excellence	9.95	
	Hundredfold	7.95	
	It's Not Working, Brother John!	8.95	
	John Avanzini Answers Questions	6.95	
	Powerful Principles of Increase	8.95	
	Stolen Property Returned	5.95	
	The Wealth of the World	6.95	
	War on Debt	7.95	
	Rapid Debt-Reduction Strategies	12.95	
	The Victory Book	14.95	
	Have a Good Report	8.95	
	Subtotal		
	Less 10% Discount		
	Shipping & Handling		2.00
	Total Enclosed		

(   ) Enclosed is my check or money order made
       payable to **HIS Publishing Company**

Please charge my: (   ) Visa   (   ) MasterCard

(   ) Discover   (   ) American Express

Account # ⬚⬚⬚⬚⬚⬚⬚⬚⬚⬚⬚⬚⬚⬚⬚⬚

Expiration Date _____ / _____ / _____

Signature_____

To assure prompt and accurate delivery of your order,
please take the time to print all information neatly.

Name_____

Address_____

City_____State_____Zip_____

Area Code & Phone (_____)_____

Send mail orders to:

HIS Publishing Company

P.O. Box 917001

Ft. Worth, TX 76117-9001

I WANT TO HELP YOU WIN YOUR WAR ON DEBT!

It has taken a year of hard work and now all of the material for the Debt Free Army is ready to be placed in your hands.

Enlist Today And The Following Materials Will Be Immediately Sent To You:

YOUR PERSONAL ONE-OF-A KIND BATTLE PLAN PORTFOLIO WHICH INCLUDES:

A large 12-place library-style audio cassette binder. •Your Battle Plan Notebook with 12 full-color dividers designed to index over 250 pages of Debt-Free Strategies. •"The First Thirty Days To Victory" – a comprehensive "Master Plan" designed to help you become debt free. •The Debt Free Army Ammunition. Your first monthly audio tape of insight, inspiration, and motivation. This is a personal one-on-one tape you will receive from Brother John each month.

GOD WANTS YOU TO BE DEBT FREE!

Now... through the Debt-Free Army you can put His plan for your Debt-Free life-style into action.

As a member of the Debt-Free Army, I will be able to personally guide you, step by step month by month, from the slavery of debt into the glorious experience of debt-free living. No matter what financial condition you're in, this strategically prepared material can take you steadily and rapidly out of debt. It's worked for others-it will work for you.

–John Avanzini

DEBT-FREE ARMY INFORMATION REQUEST FORM

☐ YES! Brother John, I believe God wants me to be debt free.

☐ YES, I want to know more about how I can be debt free! Please send my personal copy of the **DEBT-FREE ARMY** Information Brochure to the address I have indicated below:

☐ Mr. & Mrs.
☐ Mr. ☐ Mrs. ☐ Miss. _____
PLEASE PRINT

_____
MAILING ADDRESS

_____
CITY, STATE, ZIP

To RECEIVE YOUR DEBT-FREE ARMY ENLISTMENT BROCHURE MAIL THIS INFORMATION REQUEST FORM TO:	Please check age
The Debt-Free Army **John Avanzini Ministries** **P.O. Box 917001 • Ft. Worth, TX 76117-9001**	☐ 18 - to - 25 ☐ 26 - to - 39 ☐ 40 - to - 55 ☐ over 55

I WANT THE FOLLOWING STOLEN PROPERTY RETURNED:

_____

_____

_____

_____

Name _____

Address _____

City _____ State _____ Zip _____

Area code and phone _____ Birthday (Mo) _____ (Day) _____

Church Name _____ City _____